This Book Belongs To

....

....

....

....

UNDER THE SEA

ADULT COLORING BOOK

Coloring Book for Adults

An Ocean Coloring Adventure

OANCEA CAMELIA

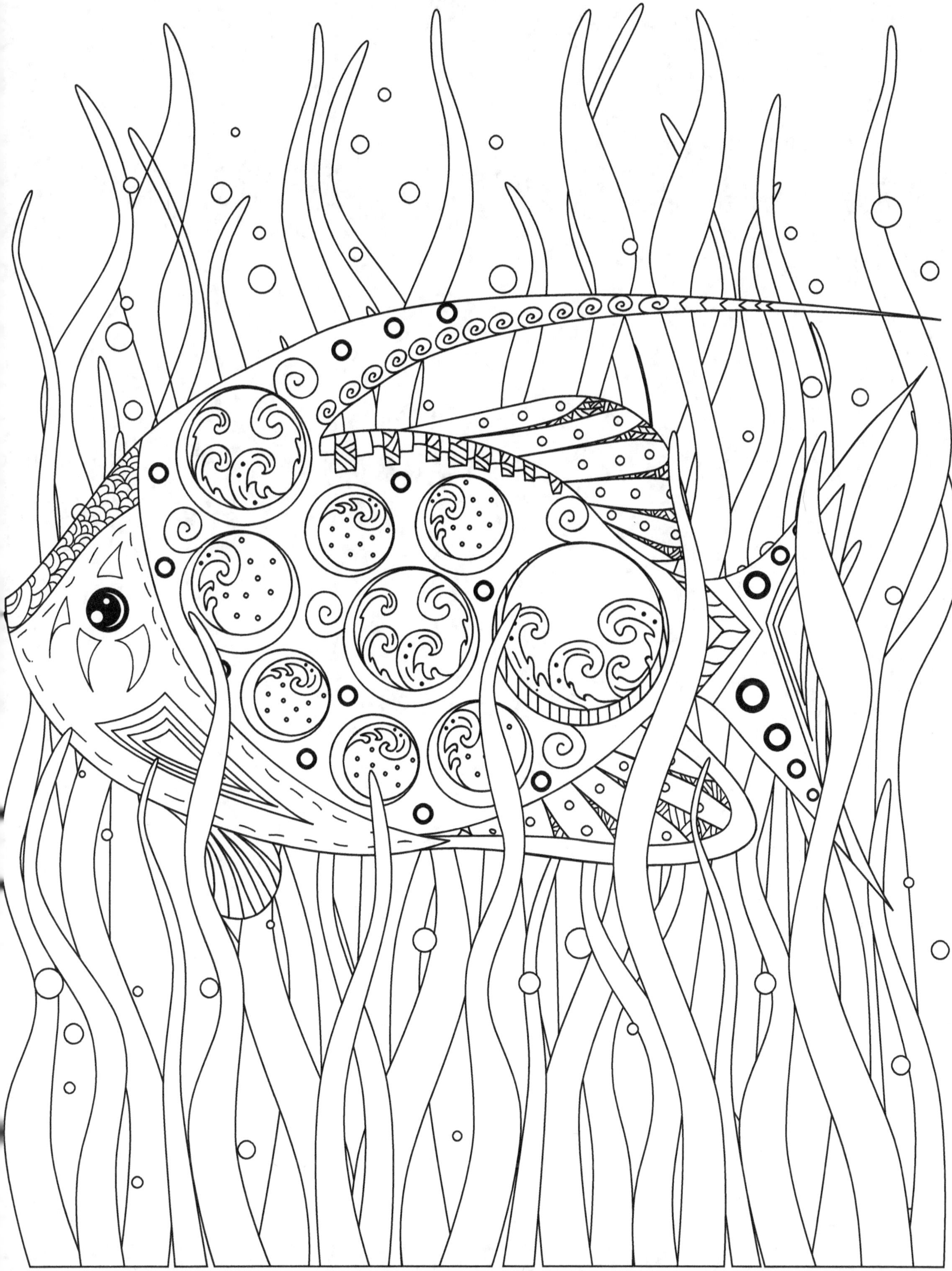

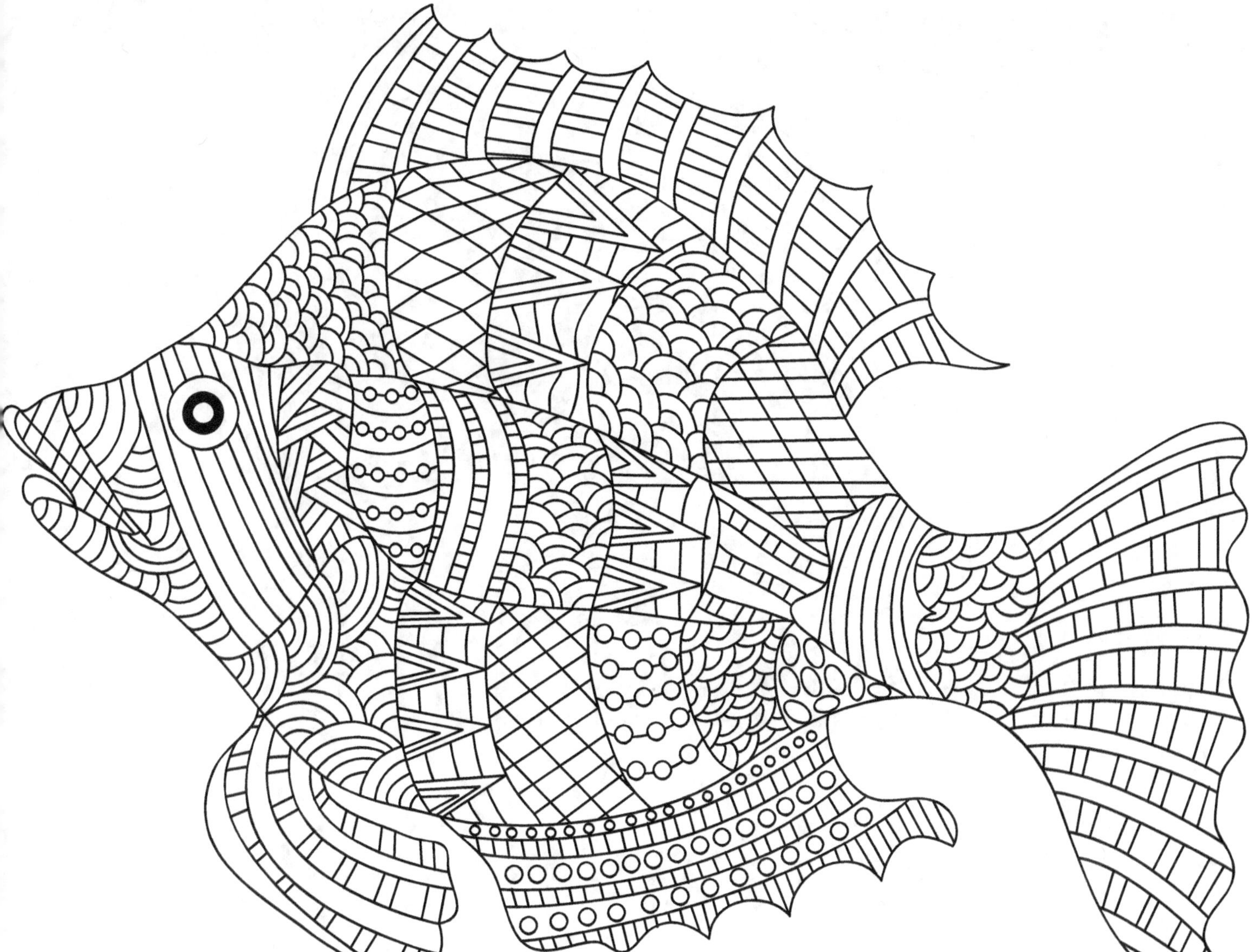

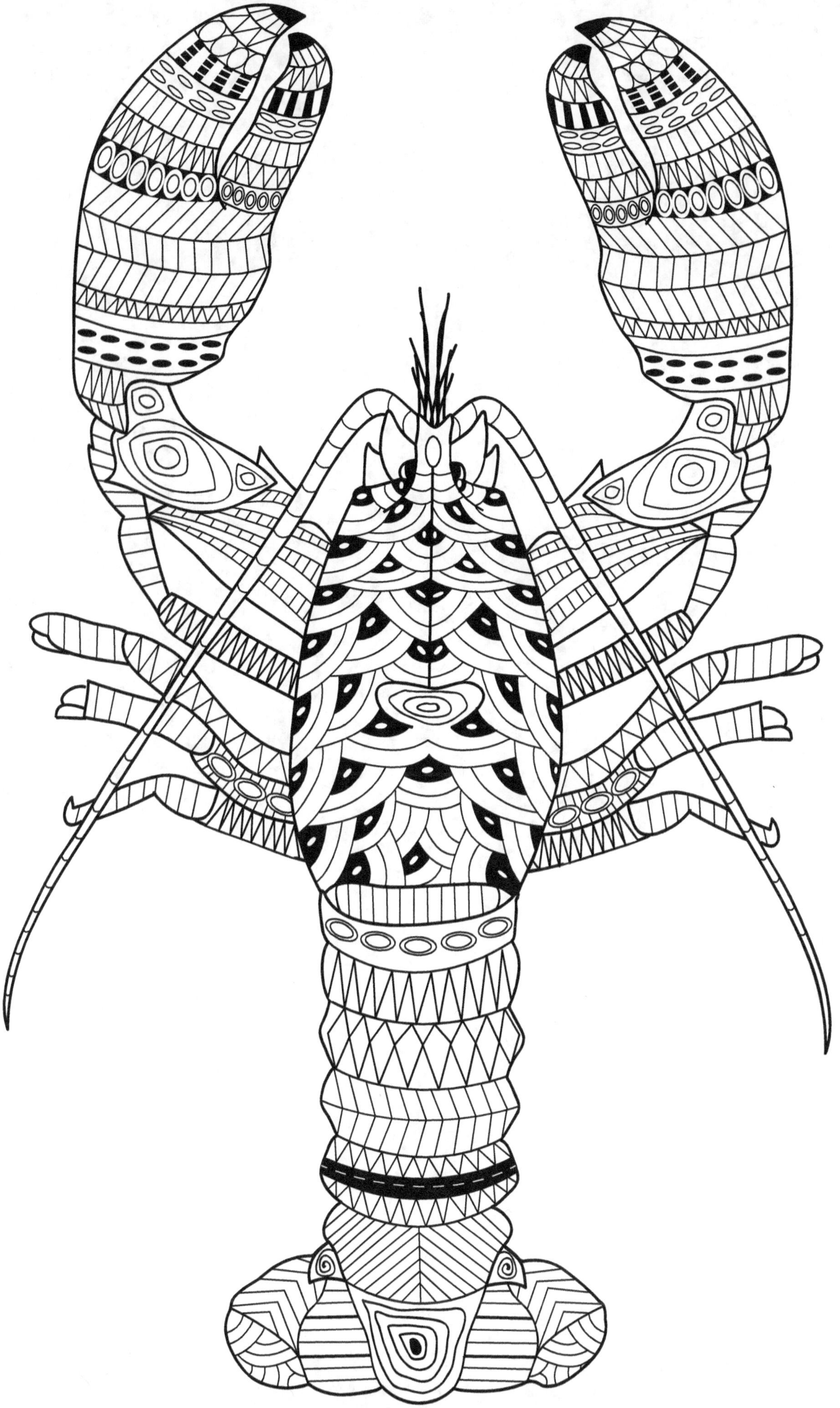

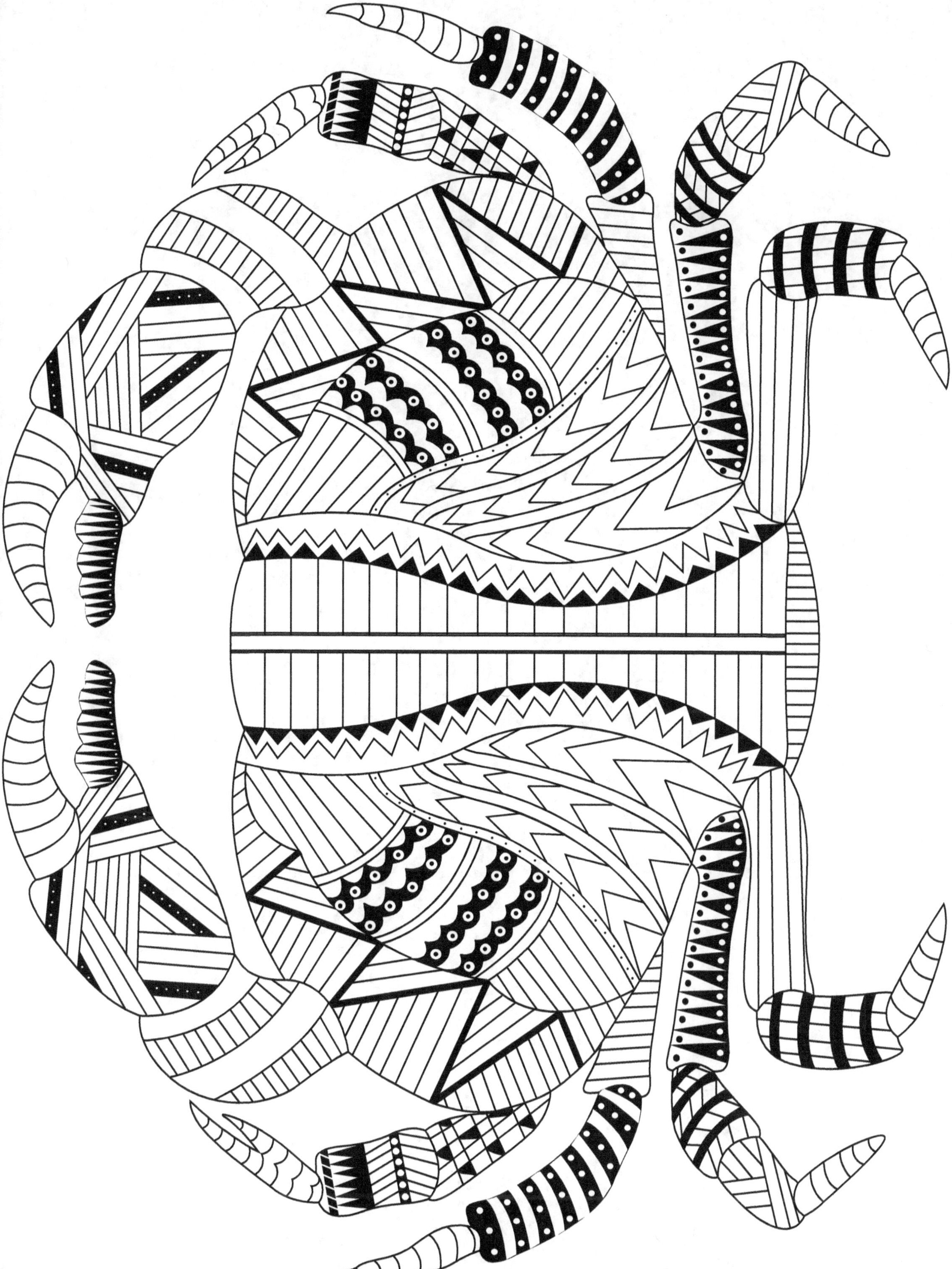

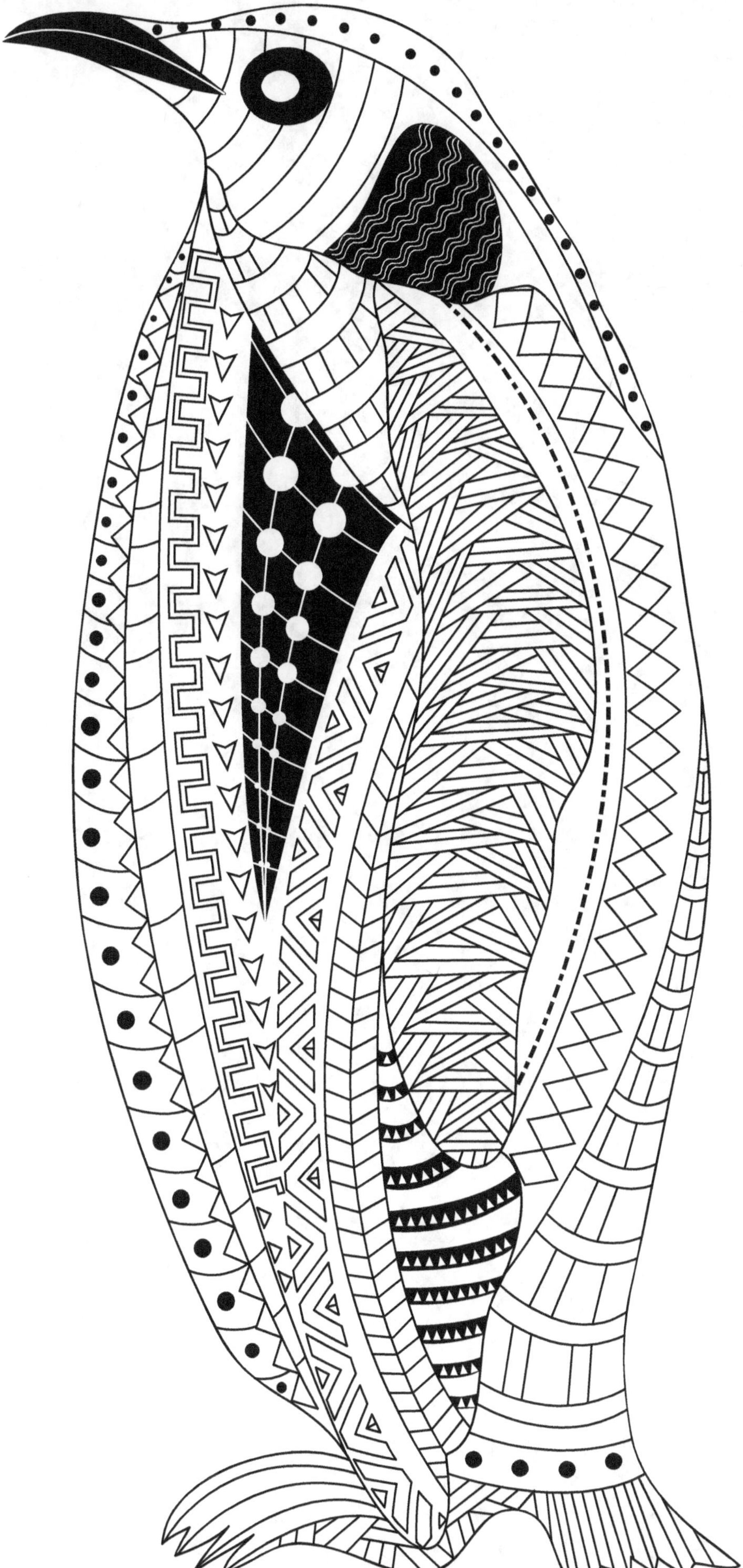

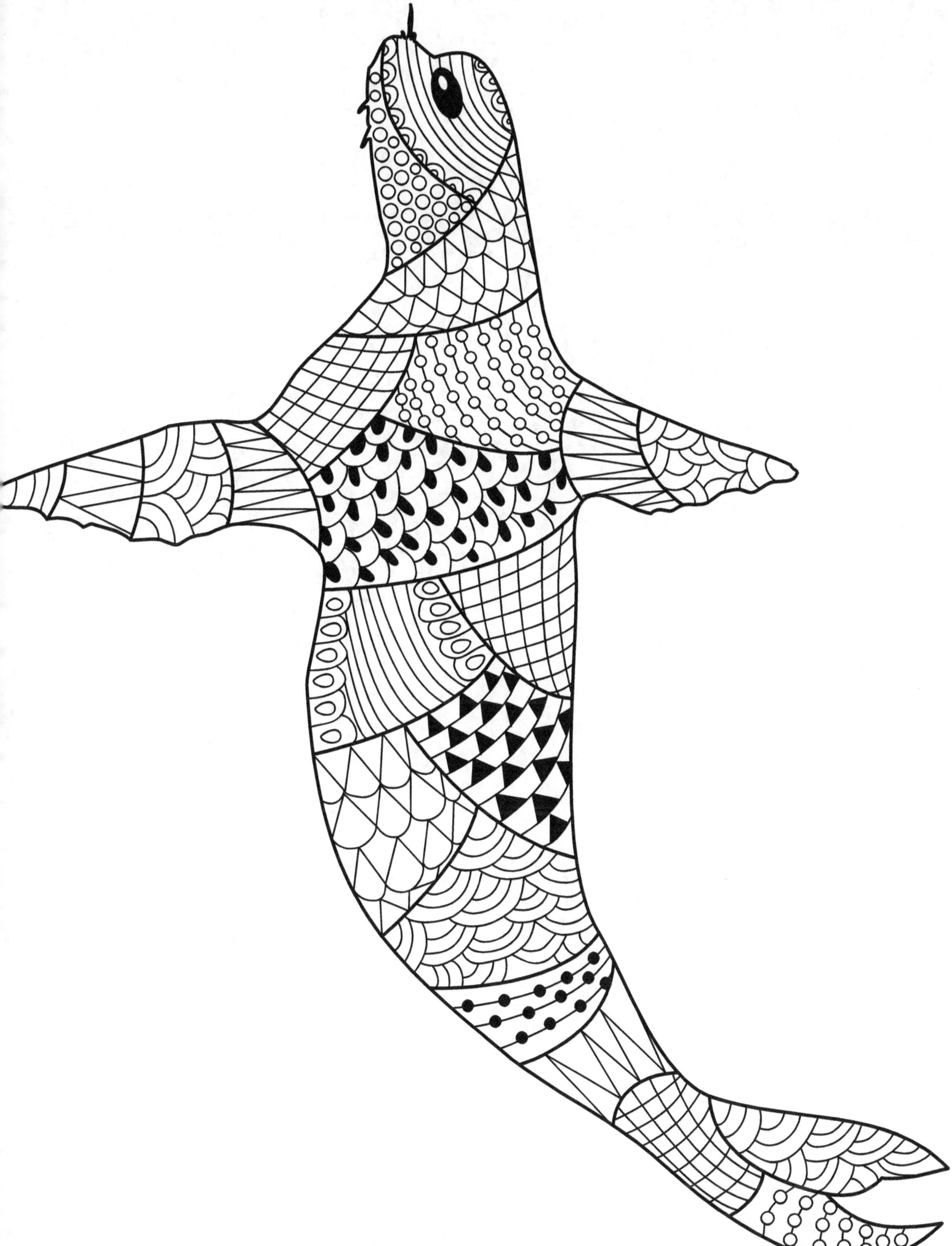

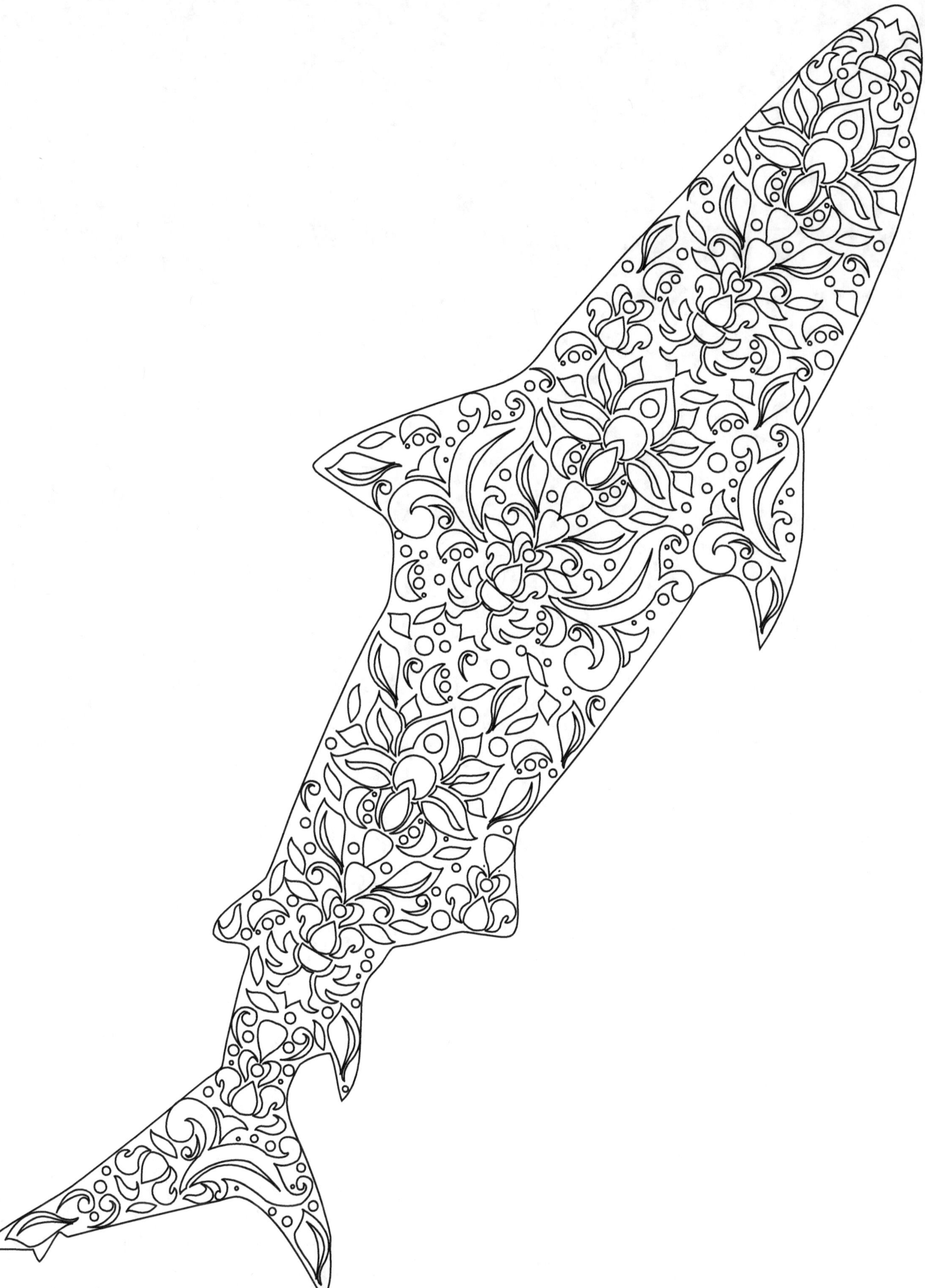

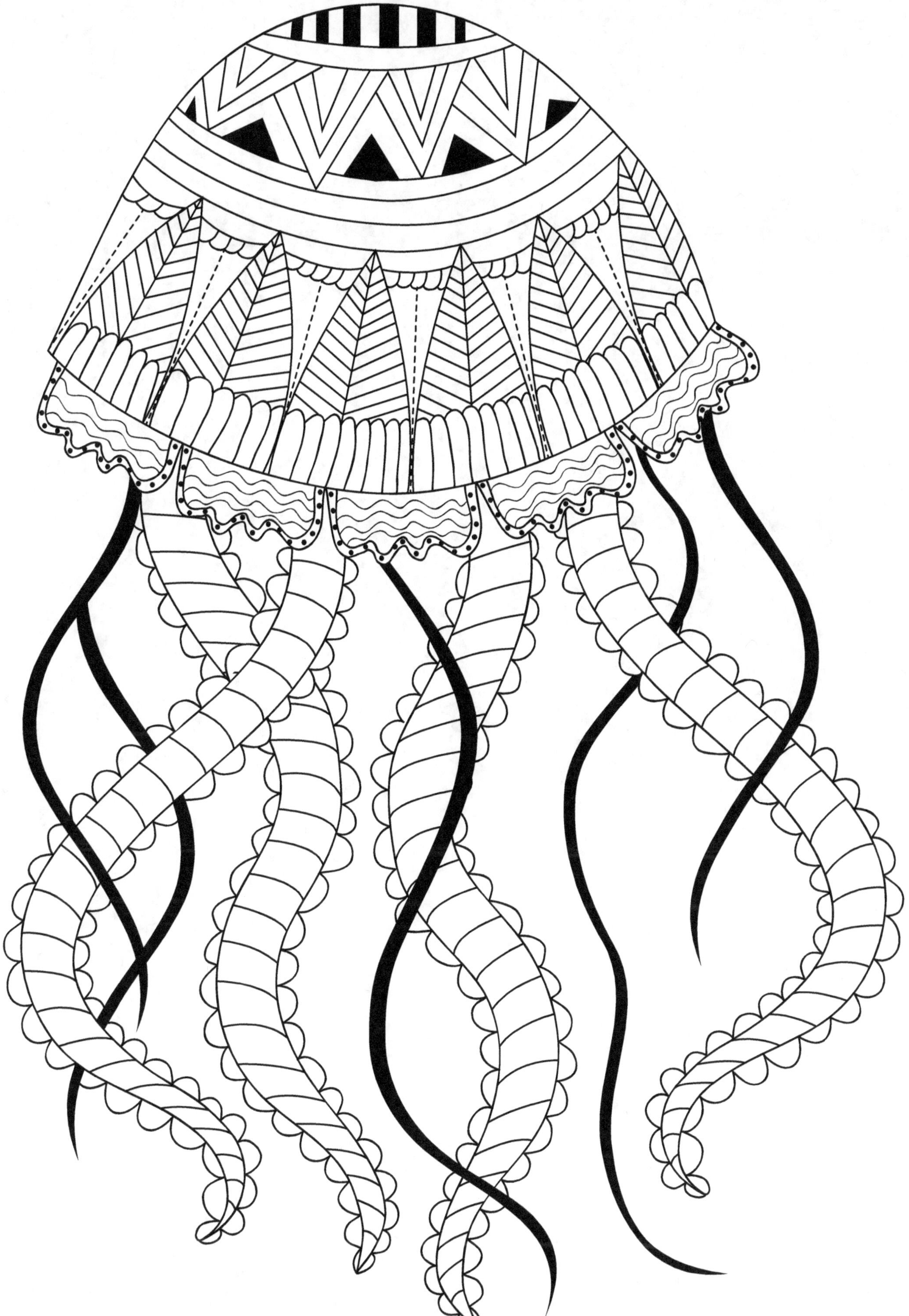